POEMS OF MANY LANDS

_TIC REFLECTIONS

Volume II

DEDICATION

*My Mother, My Wife and My Children
without whom I would not exist;
and*

*To the thousands of people
I have had the privilege of
sharing with, and those who
are and always will remain –
MY FRIENDS.*

also

*To you; my Reader:
For without you, this book
need not exist.*

POEMS OF MANY LANDS

POETIC REFLECTIONS

Volume II

RHYS OWEN

Beech Publishing House
15 the Maltings
Turk St
Alton

First Edition , 1992

ISBN 1–85736–025–7

24/2/93

Beech Publishing House
15 the Maltings
Turk St
Alton
Hants , GU34 1DL

CONTENTS
Part I

Part II

Part III

Part IV

Part V

Part VI

Poet's Note

It is for you, my reader, to decide whether my poems should flourish or wither and despair. From all my works, this book contains a selection of those that I consider to be amongst my best. As my writings span many years, I have attempted to select poems from certain geographical areas for release in different volumes.

Volume Two contains further poetic reflections of Wales and New Zealand. In addition are included poems reflecting changes of the African continent, as observed in Zambia. As promised, Volume II includes poetry, reflective of my experiences in Australia and Africa. Thoughts on Salmon Rushdie's 'Satanic Verses' are dramatic and direct. I have also included my poetry which is quite miscellaneous.

Children's Section

Part IV is dedicated to children – who are not necessarily confined to any age. I am dedicated to including a 'Young Persons' section in each volume I write.

Rhys Owen

ACKNOWLEDGEMENT

I am indebted to all that it has been my unique privilege to experience. God's gift of a receptive and perceptive mind might be mine. Born to Wales is my blessing; Sharing this blessing is a privilege: If this sharing results in the cultural advancement of nations – then this is sublimation.

Throughout my life; I have allowed my sensitivity to show recognition of others thinking, whilst adjusting, sometimes painfully, to allow them full expression. To me, observation of others reception and thought transmission, together with a mutual perception, results, so often, in comprehension and communication.

All people have so much to give; I must always adjust my antennae; my wavelengths; my frequencies – upwards never down. Each individual has his id; his ego; thankfully unobtainable by me. If, throughout my travels in this world, I have learnt, through sharing thoughts with thousands, just one iota of each mind from which I've momentarily 'collected' one thought, idea or secret – then I am indeed a very wealthy man. I find, at times, perception agonising, as I dread that I may impose my thoughts – unless occasion presents itself – on others. I thrive on empathy, rapport.

Through these tools I can build; these have been the seeds from which my writings have grown. It is for you, my reader, to decide whether my poems should flourish; or wither and despair. From all my works, Volume II contains a selection of those that I consider to be amongst my best, is complementary to Volume I and anticipates Volumes III and IV.

Empathy, results from sharing. I owe so much to so many, including those who have unwittingly allowed me to observe their humanity. This observance is seldom intentional, but as a scene captured by an artist, my scenario also exists; my duty; indeed my urgent desire, is to convey that 'reflection' to paper, – hence: "Poetry of Many Lands", "Volume Two".

I think it would be remiss of me not to acknowledge in the broadest terms the following, to whom I am indebted and give thanks:
TO THE THOUSANDS OF PEOPLE I HAVE HAD THE PRIVILEGE OF SHARING WITH, AND THOSE WHO ARE AND ALWAYS WILL, REMAIN MY FRIENDS.

Rhys Owen

ABOUT THE POET AND HIS POETRY

Rhys Owen

Born in Wales; raised in Wales. A childhood spent in Llandeilo, in the heart of the County of Carmarthenshire (now in Dyfed) in West Wales; the site of Dynevor Castle. Rhys Owen's home; an intriguing house – 'The Moreb', set beside the trout fisherman's idyllic river Towy, eighteen miles from Dylan Thomas's Laugharne.

Rhys Owen encapsulates all that is intrinsically Welsh, applying a distinct, yet subtle, completely unique insight into various aspects of life in New Zealand, Wales and other countries.

"Poems of Many Lands – Poetic Reflections" (Vol. I) represented a conceptual literary first for New Zealand – first published in Wellington and now by Beech Publishing House in England. A unique collaboration of thoughts reminiscent of the traditional links between these two beautiful "Lands of our Fathers". There are also poetic reflections of African scenarios and a "Children's Section".

No poetry, reflective of Wales or New Zealand's life style, would be complete without mention of politics, people, places, religion – and rugby. Blessed with magnificent countryside, both countries abound with mountains, forests, trout streams and craggy coastlines. Inherent to the Welsh – the Rhondda Valleys; the mountains; the coal face and a restrained insularity, resulting from Whitehall's political domination. Inherent to the Kiwi, a tough sense of independence, necessitated by its geographical location and similarly small population.

New Zealand and Wales, both share a resolute determination to be themselves. It is in recognition of this spirit, that the poet, unashamedly created these "Poetic Reflections", in literary recognition of the "Hwyl" and "Mana" of these two peoples respectively. This second volume adds 'Reflections' on Australian and African peoples., as well as further poetic works.

Of interest to Rhys Owen's younger readers are a selection of delightful poems hopefully giving encouragement for their readers to voluntarily seek solace in verse in their growing and adult years.

As promised, <u>VOLUME TWO</u>, which you now hold in your hand, contains a miscellany of poems, which again include poetry of Wales and New Zealand. Also contained, as promised, are reflective poems of Zambia, Africa; N. Australia and reflections of religion, politics and Salmon Rushdie's 'SATANIC VERSES'.

NOTA BENE

Unlike many who have simply 'travelled' – Rhys Owen has the advantage of living and working a year or two at a time with for example, the Zambian people in three remote areas of Africa; travelling in the Congo; working with his forest workers – again in Africa – for a further year.

Not only did Rhys Owen live in Australia for eight years, but administered and taught in a remote, outback school, shared dialogue with newly arrived Asian and European migrants in Darwin, Northern Australia at the time of Cyclone Tracey and liaised closely with the Aborigines and their problems in Northern Arnhemland.

These and many other experiences shared by Rhys Owen through his writings are unique in that he enabled each experience to help consolidate the next – with some substance.

"Glimpses" of peoples other than your own nation or race, can lead to damaging misinterpretations, if some basic research is not undertaken.

More details of Rhys Owen's experiences follow in "The Poet – A Silhouette".

An avid traveller, Rhys Owen first ventured from his native Wales in 1969, whilst a student at King's College, Caerdydd. As a 'Cultural Exchange Student' he was to glean his initial glimpse of foreign life;,in West Germany, and experienced the thought provoking experience of standing on the border between "Eastern and Western" Europe.

Acceptance into the British Mercantile Marine as a Cadet, two years later, saw Rhys Owen travelling to Brazil, Algeria and behind the 'Iron Curtain' to Poland. The voyage through the Baltic is reflected in the poem "Baltic Lament", illustrative of the keen intellect of the younger Rhys Owen. Becoming acutely aware of the restrictions imposed on his literary work and intellectual ambitions by pursuing life as a seaman, Rhys Owen "signed off" and recommenced his studies.

In order to finance his ambitions, Rhys Owen chose to join a gang of Welsh forestry workers and was employed by the British Forestry Commission. For two years he experienced the comradeship, and frustrations, of tough, resilient men who spent their working lives planting, lumberjacking and maintaining Welsh hillside forests, plantations and nurseries.

Rhys Owen's love of the Arts, involved him in a daily three fold experience. Clambering onto the back of a Forestry Commission truck in the early morning; rehearsals and live theatre or rehearsals in the evening, and study, often until the early hours of the following morning. Perhaps the triumph of Rhys Owen's modest theatrical endeavours was when he successfully played the part of 'Demetrius', in William Shakespeare's "A Midsummer Night's Dream", at the Prince of Wales Theatre, Cardiff.

In 1964, Rhys Owen was selected by the British Voluntary Service Overseas Organisation (V.S.O.) for service in the Zambian Youth Service (Z.Y.S.) in a newly independent Zambia, Central Africa. This service involved teaching and instructing young Africans, of many different tribes and clans, as a Staff Officer, in support of a Zambian Government initiative to encourage a "...cohesive national spirit of brotherhood" amongst its young people. Men between the ages of eighteen and twenty–eight, of whom had been trained or participated in subversive anti-colonial activities, were encouraged to voluntarily enlist into the Z.Y.S., which opened camps in remote Zambian locations. The politically charged atmosphere and violence attributed to the Service made its impact on the young Rhys Owen as did exchanges of communication relating to the emotions and ambitions of his Zambian friends. The nature of the situations that Rhys Owen had found himself in, at 20 years of age, were suggestive of countless ponderable hours; whether on watch at sea; working in the Welsh hillsides or teaching British history to a group of Zambian nationalistic fanatics in remote African locations.

Political overtones of Rhys Owen's work in Africa were accentuated when Rhys Owen was offered, and accepted, a challenging position as a Field Manager, responsible for the welfare and work of one hundred and thirty Africans and one Italian. Responsibility for these men, at 20 years of age, and the hundreds of hours spent in lonely forest areas of Zambia, left its impression on Rhys Owen's receptive mind.

Rhys Owen now returned to Wales and entered the Caerleon College of Education (University of Wales School of Education) in Gwent.

He graduated as a high school teacher in 1970.

Whilst a student, many months of vacations saw Rhys Owen working as a drayman for Rhymney breweries, delivering barrels of beer to pub cellars in the Rhondda and Rhymney Valleys and manning the spraying platform of a tar truck – which according to friends would have been Rhys Owen's "blackest hour".

After completion of his studies and one year's mandatory teaching in Wales, Rhys Owen was recruited by the New South Wales Department of Education. After one year's service in Sydney, he was promoted to become a sole charge teacher of an outback school. He later pioneered ESL and TEFL evening and daytime educational classes in Darwin, Northern Australia, (then the Northern Territory) and then worked with the Aborigines of Arnhemland, Northern Australia, as an Adult Aboriginal Education Project Officer. These two latter positions eventuated in Rhys Owen being offered a public service position, on secondment from the Commonwealth Teaching Service, to the Australian Department of Education in Canberra, as a Project Officer. In this position, Rhys Owen was involved with professional writing in preparation of educational material for the Language Teaching Branch (L.T.B.), which worked in close liaison with the Department of Foreign Affairs.

Whilst on holiday in Fiji in 1978, Rhys Owen met and later married his captivating wife, Nisha. Shortly after their marriage Rhys Owen and his wife holidayed in New Zealand and fell in love with the country. By a remote chance, Rhys Owen called in at the Auckland office of the Education Department and, after an informal discussion with a senior Education Officer, he was encouraged to join the New Zealand teaching profession. After formalities were completed, Rhys Owen commenced a New Zealand teaching career and was quickly to become a permanent high school teacher, whilst a master at Wellington College.

Rhys Owen and his wife are raising two healthy boys, both born in New Zealand. In their ten years of permanent residence they have travelled extensively throughout the country. The degree to which Rhys Owen has travelled is significant enough, but since his childhood days, observing the Towy Valley in Wales from his 'Moreb' garden seat – he has written poetry, over the years. Many unique experiences and encounters find their way into Rhys Owen's work. Some appear in this book, Volume Two; many others will appear in future volumes in 1991 – all are 'Poetic Reflections' – captured in a way that is – the literary style of Rhys Owen.

After absences of more than 19 years from his homeland, Rhys Owen is back in Britain and presently teaching in a State High School.

"Poetic Reflections – Poems of Many Lands" <u>Volume II</u>
is a selection of Rhys Owen's work.

BRIEF GLIMPSES OF THE SELECTED POEMS
IN THIS BOOK (Vol. II) POETRY OF MANY LANDS

A New Zealand Dell

'Bracken – brittle, brown and beaten
Trees – wistful, woeful, waiting, watching.
Opossum seeks its source of food,
Bush–rats scavenge like the gulls.
This; nature's test – so totally profound'.

Capital Intruders – Caerdydd

'This capital, this Cardiff, my demonical demise,
She shrinks before my glassy stare:
Enveloped in a coal face of surprise,
Her dotage – her hinterland alone, to love and care'.

Perpetrators

'Rushdie; may Allah tolerate the mention of
Satan's earthly name – you have evoked wrath afar.
"We gave Jesus, son of Mary, clear signs, and
We strengthened Him with the Holy Spirit".
You, Rushdie have mocked the very fabric of the Holy'.

Gove – N.T. Australia

'Not satisfied – hyperactive Aboriginals disgorge
                                        western swill.
Khaki garbed; silver epauletted crown – buttoned whites,
Toss bags of stinking, human flesh aboard
Polished Toyotas, wire cages abaft, not for rabid dogs.

Zambians Under the Sun

'Attitudes; some wanton, some forlorn,
Negative; negarious; oft' times inborn
Fortune seems to run with all that's new,
Our battle seems to rest with Afrikaners charm,
Their boorish wit seems to cause security from harm'.

Poles (Children's Poem)

'The world is round
That's quite profound
For there is a CIRCLE
All around.

THOUGHT ETERNAL

Man's Id: is infinite

Man's Ego: is finite

The Paradox, that is man:— is the Conundrum

Rhys Owen

Each and every soul in heaven is
Worth every soul in hell,
'Mongst morning mist the holy cross,
Seems merely just a shell.

Each time a ghost is nigh,
Its presence may be heard,
Aspire we to the holy ghost,
Our wonderings quite absurd.

As often as the cock crows thrice,
Aside the Holy Grail,
We of substance may decide,
Our future's wan and pale.

Victoria Falls

I shall not be missed a while, perchance to dream,
My little world now, seems eloquent, serene;
All hope of lust and danger withered, strewn,
Like dreams of sombre, lifeless tombs:

>   Here in life's belly I enjoy
>   Life's sweet awakening,
>   Its emergence from its Troy.

This posthumous fortune of a Fall;
A pouring forth; a gush; a frightening pall,
All dignity seems washed – dispersed,
Surrounding air gulps spray, with unsolicitated thirst:

>   Mighty in its dignity of fall,
> A desert dweller watches waste – appalled.

In all its rousing, glorious, prodigious cascade,
A nation's lifeline tumbles, rants and raves.
Each prismatic droplet, promises anew
A better life to all – not just the white skinned few:

>   Perhaps in tumult, this – a nation's blood,
> Persistent in existence, will be better understood.

FOREST FOOD – MY LOGGING MEN IN MISAKA FOREST ZAMBIA

Raw flesh, rotted in a day of heat,
Roasted over fire now, this feast,
Closes off each enigmatic day.
Men, tired – Solo chain saws still ringing in
Saw – dusted ears; the dull thud of
Log on log; tree felled on tree;
Trucks clatter; drivers curse as gears
Spring, indentured to their brassy axles.

Smoky fire is lit, neath a hapless tree.
Mutende, follows vicious bees to hive aloft;
The tree; ripped down; wild mellifluous honey trickles forth.
Each Bemba; eyes transfixed –
Buries hand and scoops out nectar.
Bees and food now gorged – handfuls
Squashed in gaping mouth within a flash,
Whilst Solo saws spit, declutched on forest floor.
Rancid smoke and flame,
Kick out from blue – hot vents.

Honey bees digested with the sting,
Slip down the inured gullet.
No discerning palette here;
Zambian ground, bordering with its recent past.
Union Jack, now lowered from freedom's view;
St George, Patrick, Andrew; lost
In laterite covered graves anew – swamped in dambo's depths

3

BRITISH DIPLOMACY

Zambia

Nkonde calls for tea; bone china rings;
Black face confronts white – both quizzical in an
Awkward way. We don't like spies.
We know what you're doing,
You are C.I.A.

The confirmation he seeks will never be.

Deportation arranged; friends will help me out;
My contacts are the highest. Just get out.
Silence is loud.
Slurps of English Breakfast; tinkle of silver spoon;
Cracks of digestive – the black proclamation seems complete.

British diplomat arrives, smiles, chats.
My promotion at Fort Jamieson is confirmed,
My future now secured by devious deeds.

Hope now for eternal bliss: death;
This the daily toil for a system
Unrelenting in its fundamental gloat,
Seeing future hopes for glory not yet
Found in crevices of vacant minds.

So we do seek this cantilevered life;
This often sways between
An interforce, obscuring all in
Unthinkable alien ways, a mangrove swamp of ethnic
Comparison; opaque yet ingenious.

Distinguished only by some simple train of thought,
So oft denied by pilgrimage to lesser fields;
Distinguished only by some distant offering of
Profanity anew – we utter resolutions to the
Black man's tomb.

We see some nocturnal difference
In our reference to the moon; Soliloquy, resemblance
Of some effigy of thought – dismal now; protruding in
This excellence of yet another careless vision
Seemingly remote – quite undistinguished by profanity;
Quite lost by pressures, interwoven by a literacy
Of subsequent tribal blasphemy anew.

PROVOKED THOUGHTS

Africa: your nights illuminate my mind.
That convection, radiation of the day,
Amethyst planets, their minions dancing polkas 'round the void:
Crescendos dazzle, quite hideous, noxious weed,
Even in death, its clarity of design seems
Fitting to some seemingly simplistic plan of logic.
Hopes revived by the birth; of one nostalgic star,
Seemingly oblivious, suspended in the black void of
Absorption of so many rays of hope; trust;
No dapple grey; no uncertainty, a bland vindication that
The majesty of the Seat of Heaven may be there.

Within each thought, each mental probe,
Comes a reflective thought; a feeling of remorse; deft
In its analogy as a temporal mass – moving, outwards; pressing;
Canker seems to grip – each finger tenuous,
Some serial thought; some epitaph to doom,
Beauty of balance; poise; equilibrium,
This brilliant fulcrum seems a balance so profound
Between Black and White, this control –
Nature's simple laws, proclaim the value difference from
Conception of universal perpetuity: This silent, strident
Group of forces – balanced yet too vast for comprehension.

Prolonged discussion leads to understanding,
Oft in the heat of moment, so passionate to an
Infinite degree, some unique dialogue – some confirmed
Interpretation, hopeful of obtaining sustance through degrees.

6

DEATH OF A CHILD

My camp is entered from the south;
Ponda; arms like flails; teeth reflective of my headlights flare.
Hard hat – at absurd angle on forehead, misplaced, odd;
Logging book still protruding from his pocket;
Mutende's wife's child is very sick.

My Land Rover – ten anxious silent folk aboard – drives south,
The cab seats four, Mafasi – silent infant on breast;
Other's dust kicks up fogs of grit; the night boils;
A sweet stench mingles with stale sweat;
"En a musha steric bwana, En a musha steric!" (please be quick)

Ghoulish hospital; Rhodesian Sister instantly
Proclaiming death? – The mother is admonished, severely,
Directed back from whence she comes.
A wail: whispers merge with silhouettes of shadowy night.
Death – its presence avericiously admires the hopeless scene.

Ponda Mwale; army style; decrees a coffin must be made.
The Rover returns; black faces adopt monastic form and chant;
Tears flow freely from sunken, doubtful eyes;
A charismatic, undenied sadness reflects a universal, tacit thought –
The seemingly pointless existence of a human, infant form.

Despite all; loved; now buried; forever gone.
Charon's boat may never know its melancholic loss.

ZAMBIA YOUTH SERVICE LUCKA, ZAMBIA
(Director's Office)

Nkonde; his Lusaka office brisk; 'Whitehall style',
Macdonald – brusque; knew the inference of this blackman's tone,

Ibraheim was curt, abrupt – fully understood by
Stubborn, canny Scot, with an Africa to design.

With some perception, Scot aligns with
Nkonde's traits – his zealous avarice, political demise.
White antipathy; racial antinomy; emolument.
Scot's travels would patronise the dead.

Myself, Commandant now, the blacks
Repulsed; not receptive of clumsy politicing,
Subservient this role; subversive of a kind,
No Bwana yet; untimely sacrifice, might yet be mine.

Discretionary chats, so impressionable to some;
Suggestions of decay of this democratic Service –
Some Nazi, nonchalant, arrogant, spearhead;
A massive, poignant tool for abuse and convenient discontent.

ZAMBIAN AVARICE

Culled of our fractious feelings,
We fail to stray anew from languages feigned
With fear; feelings frail, aye, fronts for depths,
Concealed beneath our seldom heard remarks,
Hidden in symbiotic, bereft signals, of constancy inherent,
Indeed wrathful, in their camouflaged Zambian zeal.

Innermost, through collusion so pliant;
Zambians must achieve; low demise, typecast,
Where greedy minds envisage prisms; colour; spectres eyes;
Felines grab with claws some tabby sneak,
Each in favour with a catch.
Now we plunder on; reckless is our spirit now;
Cautious our ineptitude to smooth away the rift.

Zambia: its colloquial chasms deep.
Its squalor, its benign majesty, its cold sun:
That native; that Bemba; that bloodied Zambesi;
Uncanny touch of baboon's filthy avarice.
Vultures circle, homing in on fetid prey;
Cacophony arrested; apprehended; temporarily disavowed –
Huts askew – reminders these of cankerous, colonial skins.

At speed – the nations wheels renew their lust.
White almost gone or turned to dust,
Misaka's revenge for ripping, raping, rasping saws;
Freedom, Quatcha! – now within their powerful jaws.

9

BANK OF VICTORIA FALLS, ZIMBABWE

Baboons scratch and tear ticks from ugly flesh;
Frightened chatterings – yet fastidious in their perpetual preening;
Victoria's emblazoned cascade; prismatic droplets – mesh,
Irridescent; scintillating; soaked; spectrum blazes colour to the scene.

Through this Zambia's urgent aorta, a quittance quite quixotic,
Quizzical, saturating spray, casting its quotidian misty spell
On Zulu from the south; Bemba from the north;
This new nation's emigre; haematic draught;
Haemorrhaging into lands of racial hell.

A WHITE MAN'S HAVEN
Zambian Clubs and Pubs

Bedford bludgeons through banal bush,
Shocks screeching, chasms opened by tropic rain,
Termites work their tunnels; Mambas spit, retreat and hide.
Dambos, double bass frogs, echo their indignant demise, as
Leo's animation listens attentively to Springbok's
Defenceless, hopeless presentation; this defendant of a bloody feast.

Hapless Zambians; conversation disgorges
Acceptance of Africaner's wit; respect far more than
Surface deep; Only a brave elongated needle would
Ply,;probe; beneath this corruptible, defensive, armoured den
Hiding; etching – never feasible; darning – never time.
He must pack his swag and return.

Zambians, their native ears attuned to huntsman's
Sounds; smells; sharp senses, flashing midnight eyes
Around the common sounds of miner's brassy bars.
Dramatic tales of local exploitation,
Insane profanities; the Zambians alert for
Any exposure, slap deportation orders on 'unwelcome guests'.

Free of filth and unguided verbiage,
Zambia loses one more skilled artisan of ore.
Surely his now to exploit and use,
The final bridge more than the chasm
There before; graveyards, in Capetown, Hull, Glasgow,
Cluttered with the colonial ghosts of empire.

ZAMBIAN INDEPENDENCE
REFLECTIONS

Seldom is heard a passive thought,
That tacit communication between compatible minds.
People of substance ever watchful of this independence; lost;
Flighty spirit seems remiss; sentiment otherwise
Directed at some distant freak, an unknown purpose.

Where else would petty reasoning be allowed,
This – A klaxon of alert awareness,
Otherwise destroyed in burial grounds of hell;
Distraught but not forever lost in crevices of minds,
Concealed in a slatternly abyss of temporal powers.

Laid aside are 'independence' thoughts;
Appearing distant – yet the Union Jack is dipped;
Perhaps the feelings of this eerie time are silent now,
The Whiteman's grip: diluted, weakened;
This reversal of his role seems quite complete.

EN ROUTE TO SOLWEZI, ZAMBIA

Silver dawn: filibustering looming sky,
Rain withheld by luck, not natural design.

Slated, distant, misty horizons,
Concurrent with Zambian roads – a slurry of treacled laterite;
This potpourri of transportational aid.

The African wrestles with this apologetic track,
As bouncing Bedford growls and grovels in agony.

Shocks, pounded to the epitomy of questionable design,
Young men, under canvass, in the back.

Cheering, whooping political slogans, shrieked at every lurch;
Soaked but never saddened by this wild affray.

Enjoyment – sheer ecstacy – this a gigantic leap,
Yet another, ex–colonial, happy, happy naive day.

Preambles these of Solwezi's calm demise,
A nation's gateway to eternal bliss and hope;
Brothers under one sun of quiet surprise
With freedom of a kind some have eloped.
Their ransom will be paid in cupric terms;
Each Zambian will toil – and sometimes learn.

This world's a bitter vetch for many zealous hopes,
Zambia, now with destiny – its future has eloped.

Attitudes; some wanton, some forlorn,
Negative; negarious; oft' times inborn.
Fortune seems to run with all that's new,
Each change of mind is open to review.
Our battle seems to rest with Afrikaners charm,
Their boorish wit seems to cause security from harm.

For whites; blacks are simply pathways to the gold.
The diamonds; Their fingers pave the way, until it's sold.

ALGIERS ARRIVAL
(1960)

My ship, relieved of Atlantic, now steams
Joyously into Mediterranean, its course from
Brazilian waters now patrolled, arrives in
Africa midst cacophonies of vibrant Arabian sounds.

De Gaulle's faceless minions, astride armoured cars.
Impervious to the patient wails of supplicatory, gregarious,
Muslims, wait 'mongst stinking, testy camels,
Their ewers and pitchers riding aloft.

Traffic assumes a wreckless, impassioned stream;
Thrusting through wretched, aromatic Casbah streets,
Ripping, threshing relentlessly the parched, arid air apart;
Motorists intent on murder, suicide, in simultaneous hit.

Complacent of surrounding chaos,
Searing tyres, violent tempers, taut, twisted nerves.
Pedlars – their sanctimonious trinkets prodigiously displayed,
Sit, cross–legged, smoking hookahs – oblivious of the day.

ARRIVAL AT FORT JAMESON

Colonial surburban sprawl, spreadeagled, mosaic,
Avenues, streets, clubs – the paraphernalia of
A wasted concept, now saddened by historical demise.
Roman walls 'mongst verdant English countryside – morose,
Grey, foreboding, threatening through their incongruous presence.
In this volatile land, Malawi breathing close,
The British bwana's house, his boy, present; mefasis patient;
All undecided where their future lies.

A hostel – red bricked, brass, glass white paint,
Minions brisk, polite, trained. Police: rank badges
Sparkling in the sun; boots aglow with nurtured, burnished warmth.

Civil servants, their sense of urgency blunted.
Minds on careers that may have been, now
Inevitably curtailed; The familiar green and black trunk,
Dusted down, packed with white man's sentimental chattels,
Destination unsure, some forgotten aunt will bear the prize.

The urban Zambian, in this remote place smells oblivion;
Life he's learnt to accept – vapourises, never replenished,
Dissipating whilst the streets get swept
The drains cleaned, shops trade, people persevere, this
Little township exists in an ominous shadow of doubt.

BOXER'S ZAMBIAN DEATH

Yellow–black bulk is heaved across
Red laterite with apparent ease,
Flexing and tightening of lithe muscles –
Coil, recoil, coil, recoil,
This adder seemingly devoid of fatal venom.

Arrowed tongue, perpetually stabbing at some fictitious foe;
White underbelly squats on shimmering ember ground;
Lateral vision steers its beady, deathly eyes
Towards Boxer's naive, canine mask;
He Springs; Puff adder – ever ready to perform this task
Strikes death; its toxic venom taints haematic gush;
An inevitable siezure.

Boxer died that day.

A mirage shimmered; ecstatic; reflecting vectors
Off Macadam; the turns of slinky coils ahead
Entrapped; each African in squalls of acrid dust;
Red dust; hot dust; blinding dust – Zambian dust.

Fatted calves chewed the miracle of grass,
Apologies for fodder so seemingly replete,
Their bloated bodies blocked the paths;
Their woeful eyes reconciled to early death.

Twenty Zambians; that Kombi made for ten –
Now leaps along the highway; it somersaults,
Rolls down storm drain's sharply sloping sides:
A seething inferno decided their fate in wretched pall.

A DISUSED MINE
Zambian Senior Camp Officers

Sounds of drums; sequential, somewhat distant;
Yet, their rhythm appertaining to urgency,
Sitting beside that empty, ghoulish catacomb of a dead mine.
Now a bristling pot for the vigour, zeal, of this
Nation's youth; its future and its human wealth.

My lonely, drifting thoughts wander aimlessly around;
Politics, promises summarised daily, 'Actions Speak
Louder than words', this disillusioned freak of politics
Unwillingly relegated to a menial task; the second in
Command – suit, hat, carved walking stick – remonstrates.

The commandant – in elegant, dignified display, seems in command,
A black world; young white subalterns sail on diplomatic tacks,
Seldom will mistakes be understood, ammunition dumps are now
replete.
Affairs with us; diplomats are now par for course,
A triple bluff required by council, the C.I.A., as epitaphs.

Ford; Diplomatic plates aglow glides into this distant place;
A lecture: Man's landing on the Moon –
The flag to show; goodwill overflows,
Zambians see reflected their own propaganda
Tossed: seemingly oblivious, back at awe struck mouths.

19

Confrontation seems the answer to silence;
Deep, sensuous, ominous silence; a quizzical, potent,
Noisy silence – its very epoch gnawing at the
Constant battering of this prudent, insolent hell.

The African; his independence newly won;
Seeks opportunity; Dispirited distended
Bellies of the Young – their ebullient eyes transfixed
On distant horizons within their clumsy, groping grasp.

So the Zambian, somewhat pathetic, whimsical in his wily politics,
Iniquitous; undermining; volatile – yet at peace
With developments now akin to all.

So seldom so we conprehend a feline form,
Indifferent to the languid pleasures of black flesh.

REFLECTIONS
Zambia

I love the silent spate of blood,
Zambesi's waters swirl in flood,
Their passage vital, undenied,
Their message always deep; implied.

Verdant bush; prismatic spray;
Backdrops laugh in bright display.
A Bemba stares as if in trance,
His river, waltzes in stately dance.

The turmoil, wrath, despair and hope,
Remembered now by older folk,
The youth that fish these waters now,
Oblivious of Welensky's row.

Mirrored in these waters surging,
Glimpses of the Black emerging,
That quick transition to white man's styles,
Disregarding custom, heritage or trial.

A fishing party of public servants arrive,
Their picnics festooned, olives, grapes and silverside.
Suits, ties, bespectacled, neat and trim,
Laughing at thoughts of envigorating swims.

They drive the latest turbo cars,
Frequent their favourite haunts and bars,
Their human rights once brutally denied,
Zambesi cries: for this African demise.

Seldom is a time more rare,
A sequoias pearl beholden of a few,
Nothing have we that is not required of you,
Subject to momentous change, in subjective views.

Pinnacles of hope, desire and pain,
Shadows cling to aspirations vain.
Cold, calculated straddles of disdain,
Thoughts, words, dreams, themes – run randomly again.

Pleasantries, those manners of the few;
So many laws have nothing, left to say,
Each thought, each platitude seems new,
So many times continued in a simple way.

Oh! so devious are the fingers of repent,
So obvious are the themes of death;
Romance is but another bent,
Desirous in encapsulating time itself.

Peace
>Peace abounds
>>Peace this Africa
>>>Peace this transcient land
>>>>Peace – Zambian, African, unique, pure.

>>Brotherhood
>>Brotherhood idealistic
>>Brotherhood reflective of our world
>Brotherhood under one universal sun.

Co-operation.
>Co-operation excels
>>Co-operation in Peace
>>>Co-operation exists, in whole thoughts.

>>Bliss
>>Bliss is peace
>>Bliss is co-operation
>Bliss is co-operation, peace and brotherhood
>Bliss is co-operation, peace, brotherhood, idealism.

>>Zambia is bliss.

INDOCTRINATION – A PERPLEXING PARADOX
Solwezi, Zambia

To palm for favours unrealised by
These children of political abuse;
Mutende; angular of jowl – ferret faced,
Pocked skin, betraying amber, eyes,
Persuading pitiful clients of his Peking
Financed drugs, to manipulate and indoctrinate all
To the thoughts of Chairman Mao.

Charles Mufulu struggles – sedition no compromise
For this intellectual mind. His counter–productive
Countenance, a stereotype; passions locked;
Easy lives denied; White tourniquet replaced by
Black; demands now seemingly anti–climatic,
Diffused; promises plucked politically, enthusiasm
Stifled by free issues of Sheffield axe and spade.

Seldom has such doubt appeared
To coalesce; a spinnaker of time.
Oft, heights pressing seem to consecrate a doubt:
How oft does flighty bird show care,
Tamed between the rafters of despair.

We seem to falter in the path of hell,
A conquest simple in degradation,
Matter more in application –
Subjected as they are to rules of man
Fathoms deep they claim a separate clan.

This Zambia – colonial delineations on a
Parchment roll: Tribes traversed by whim of man;
Pith helmets, badges of rank, peddling profiteers –
They've left pathetic effluent now licentiously steered.

Western waste pollutes this native land;
Zambians task to use them as their ow.n.
Banks, commerce, trade inherited to bespoil,
This wild seductive land, best left alone to toil.

Maternal instinct apparent; baby eyes bulging towards day;
Gluttonous foxy smiles, hideous in their contempt –
Black victory Oh! so shallow in a hollow pre–emptive way;
A nation this in utter disarray; tattered; unkempt;
Its alms now suspended; its freedom fighters lost –
Zambesi alone makes thunderous acclaim,
The politicians not to count the cost –
The price of man's eternal struggles;
The fight and now the pain.

Baboons scratch and tear ticks from ugly flesh,
Frightened chatterings – yet fastidious in their perpetual preening;
Victoria's emblazoned cascade; prismatic droplets – mesh
Iridescent; scintillating; soaked; iris oglers steaming,
Through this – Zambia's urgent aorta, quintescence quite quixotic,
Quizzical, saturating spray, casting its quotidian misty spell on
Zulu from the south; Bemba from the north;
This new nation – emigre; haematic draught;
Haemorrhaging into lands of racial hell.

PLAYFUL AGONY – ENCOUNTER WITH A
HIPPOPOTAMUS (Zambia)

Hippo glided sedately up Misaka stream.
Grey – black this thunderous Sunday afternoon,
Pure water; its pools reflective of beasts persistent toil,
Its will to satiate its urgent need for peace.

Sticks, stones, yells, jeers – a common horde,
Entrails are hurled enthusiastically,
Grey, bewildered beast asks only for that same
Peace, that independence, his slaughterers now seem deprived.

Cut, ripped, pummelled – in agony now;
The beast, in frenzy, churns the water red –
Pink droplets land on black tattooed arms,
Backdrop of livid green bush, makes a carnival of death.

Killing complete; unlucky hapless beast is torn from
Stream's unsatisfactory mating obscurity;
Carcass is dragged, trussed and hoisted;
Adeptly skewered – and eaten without grace.

Killer dawn betray me not; suffocating
Sadist; severe mind severed oft a
Crevice crawl; Mistaken I again – my
Once seized tenacity now rampant, indeed her
Molestations yet anew; Cankerous chasms
Outwit toppling torsos of peasants,
Falling; oblivious of a stalking salutory
Shadow, shortened by this sombre, insignificant
Shunt towards another Zambian day.

Quatcha! Quatcha! by the thousand,
Betrayed youth cry aloft for Mana,
As yet unrevealed. Gone the trappings
Of a royal guard. Now disquiet; tribal
Rumblings hitherto so cunningly contained: Now their
Tremulous chords: Reverberations felt;
Ready again, they demand their right, their place,
The odours of bloody heritage perceived, smelt;
Oh – Zambian breeze, wafting, pungent, clean – aloft.

RAW MEAT
(A Zambian Hunt)

My observation of an American Tourist Party's Sport

I joined my Camp beyond the town;
The hunting party from the States,
Their punitive task to satiatingly hollow elephant;
Entrails red, to spill on Africa; militaristic skills endowed.

Eternal dollars changed eager hands that night –
Broad, brawdy, Bronxy gutteral claims
Of multifarious beasts; Seen from zooming scopes
Inviting the blind to squeeze easy triggers.

Zambia – the losers as before: My camp awaits;
No welcome – only stark uninvited greetings. My
Presence seen as imposition on this nationalistic,
Transitory life.

Hostel chefs smuggle adequate chunks of bleeding flesh;
Partially roasted now served 'mongst silver candelebra.
Starched linen, champagne – all so incongruous, almost ghoulish
In their fruit festooned presentation.

Obliging beast peers from its observatory at the gorging mess.

29

CORROBOREE
(ARNHEMLAND, NORTHERN AUSTRALIA)

Are you caught? Am I so naive?
The hefty clout of March is hence;
Each churlish hour; each offering some recompense;
I die in death; ephemeral – my life knows no reprieve;
Come, Spring; enshroud my immortal tomb –
Listen: hearten to my erstwhile conscience;
Satiate me with discontent and vengeance.

Come, Spring; born these glories of nature's womb.
Pleasures mixed with Satan's lust for hate.
We; you and I with I, and all that's you with you,
Will conquer mutual hate for tasteless, tedious, hurtful darts;
As in death I die; my life no longer waits;
A cold, glinting, gluttony of hardened glances,
Reach deepest levels of my intermittent trances.

Resplendent in a veil of compromise and fate;
I trim the sails of fortitude anew;
My ecstacy replenished, enamoured, relieved;
I see no hankering, inhuman fiend,
No grotesque epitaph to my durable but dented demise;
As silent wings of Ebony birds are preened; avaricious,
Funereal hoods, morbid masks, verdant, crimson encircled eyes,
Gloat, restless in their yielding compromise.

ABORIGINAL DEFICIT

Queensland: jackbooted representatives of the Crown,
Brass tipped heels of education's dropouts,
Crush the very truth; Black man has a right.

Kiwi's; scampering from their isles so sad;
Languish in the fatter fields of this querulous State,
On fringe of Sydney's unhappy beaches.

How cruel to teach the children Maori:
At age of reason their comprehension of
The Maori, place in Godsown is shattered.

Why can't white tenants of Australia's
Better jobs
Awake?

Never has been
Such obvious, conscious denial – oblivion of
A fate bestowed upon the naive people of outnumbered clans.

AN INCONGRUOUS SWIMMING POOL – GORE

A child sits beneath a tropic sun;
He gazes fixedly at glassed mirror that's the brine.
Reflections tend to lighten up his eyes,
Seditious are the ripples; the beckoning shore line.

Intermediate to the distant lure of nature's cooling bath,
Water pipes denote, a plastic world of Aussies whites,
A cacophony of pressure pipes and playful happy screams,
This apartheid, this separation, is a perplexing sight.

The white man's tapped spring waters
Held in holes within the ground.,
He's gone to so much trouble,
To protect his fishing grounds.

Children from Yirrkala, Arnhemland and Gore,
Avoid this insular chilly place,
To them it's alien, strange, contrived,
Belonging to some weird, ethereal race.

Like all of Gore's bestrewn profile,
This contusion adds a quirk,
Monies spent could host a Clan,
Contemptuous Aboriginal, can only grin and smirk.

MAORI – OF TWO MINDS

Embellished in an attitude of bliss; oh so
Symbolic of desert tombs; so crass; so Maori.
Hills of brittle sands; waterless – yet as fluid
As the sea; arid, yet life suporting cacti;
Seeds awaiting moisture yet ambivalent in patient
Calculus and peace; This New Zealand – so naive,
Flirts with loathsome, immoral souls, which simply breed contempt.
Man's maniacal mind; seething, somewhat; Grasping
Greedily for answers so benign. Vague,
So circumspect, yet, always with avaricious grasp.

Stake out new enterprise. Entrepreneur may
Yet work his claim. Black depths of recession, doubtful
Government promise; substantial national waste and ruin;
Broken backs of families – so naive before,
But not so ghastly, so apparent, in this Kiwi face –
As guilty buffoon and friend guffaw on trivia in this
Nation's saddened, fading backdrop. His only hope now to
Escape unharmed amongst the has beens of Hades, yet another
Aboriginal depleted of his rightful land and place.

33

A NEW ZEALAND DELL

Bracken – brittle, brown and beaten,
Trees – wistful, woeful, waiting, watching.
Opossum seeks its source of food,
Bush–rats scavenge like the gulls.
This; nature's test – so totally profound.

    Streams tumble without a care,
    Where anglers wiat to lure their fare;
    No time have human's minds to pause,
    No time to reason, search for cause.

God's own, this Shangri–la of land,
That beauty, simple it appears,
Suckles warmth and awe in Man,
He knows it's useless to compete.

    With this – nature's sometimes ghoulish plans,
    With this – God's supreme reply,
    To unbelieving souls who dare,
    Plans divine have now revealed,
    An eternity of immense appeal.

APARTHEID WITHOUT PREJUDICE
Underground Racialism

Colonial policies, vocabularies – blacktrash;
"Only good when dead". "Kaffirs naked in the sun".

Sweat oozing from open pores. Passive, oblivious silence,
One bastion, Australia, where white outnumbers black!
No hypocrisy here – Maori statistics reveal all so clinically.

Forces putrid with the White man's shame,
Tribes; Mana dissolving in the mediocrity of
New Zealand's naivety, its bankruptcy so evident.

Toil they must. White man; gross, obese;
Beer bellied wealth his only asset, his
Aspirant – no whip today, but patronising verbiage,

These men with rights, unions,
Their undenied freedom to desecrate, survive;
Have they a real place in these isolated, petty isles?

What illiteration; these outnumbered patronising pawns,
So unaware this purposeful proliferation of their land;
Now; so many; slaves to Social Welfare's promissory note.

Tenants in this multiracial little land; theirs to slyly ply
For unregistered self esteem. Perhaps their majority in prison
Cells, dole queues and educational failures, tell it all.

35

RACIAL MINORITIES

NEW ZEALAND AND AUSTRALIA

Where are the Maoris? separated by their
Own design; their clan; the Pakeha; how proud and
How convenient too.

Commissioned strident whites – The Kiwi black has little chance:
Why – even that USA; that epitomy of racial hypocrisy,
Conceded two score years ago, superficial compliance
                                                    with civil rights.

The Aboriginal is about to die: Australia's
Nhulunbuy, Yirrkala, Elco Island – witnesses to black's demise.
Vernacular signs of welcome at the airports, stations, towns –
Greet migrants – not Australia's own.

Residential signs in Aboriginal tongue – the cave paintings;
Like Maories – White man has tossed you in a rut, a groove –
Buried 'neath the langishings of time.

This is your land, in title, word and deed. Barrelled ranks of
Politicians – predominantly, – increasingly white. New
Zealanders of which you're not a part.

Like white to Red Indian, Afrikaner to Zulu, Aussie to Aboriginal
You may be the loser; at least the 'Master Folk' of
Pretoria are blatant in their stealth.

Destructive of the Union Jack, the Boston Men marched on,
Defiling; murdering millions of those red skinned folk.

Importing black's to labour on their land,
Money from those Aboriginal grounds, gave
Benevolence a chance to toss, the awesome dice of death.

36

The graft of turmoil,
Sense of serious strife.
Stringent semaphor's eclat,
Mentioning a straggled, yet synchronised scene.

This public rubbish dump of Lange's
Wasted, writhing, wriggling dream.

To those who abhor this New Zealand
We pay homage; Self destructed; aided,
Abetted by some obscene prussian effigy of
Government attrition; we see this comedy of events
Unfold; The very guise – immodest to deny our friends a place;
Permits our very conscience to live at all.

All New Zealand dies an interim, economic death,
Those plainly aware of folly, dissipate; dissolve, disencumbered,
Indeed confined; convalescent after their staggering demise;
Unable to construct a new charisma; gloating, blunting, bastardly.

That deceitful double imagery from a trained street–fighter,
Prebbles mind unflustered by contradiction, leads pointlessly.
People receive what they deserve; they also have no
Knowledge of their dissidence; that baffoon;
That clown's cunning, cauterises sobriety as silent adversaries
Of democratic ways; sneak from silhouetted shadows.

Amidst arclights with blinding, piercing glare,
Lange's barrelled torso, belies his disgusting loutish
Caricature of sixties' Beatlemania, Yoko and her fiendish
World.

It's infallible; an effigy of their time:
Welcome you to its trough of mediocrity;
Sustain a substance in your midst,
Sustain a creative attempt of conscience desire;
We bequeath a secret sanctity in which
We overwhelm a procrastinating, prosaic, purpose of mind.

So seeks this New Zealand as a compromise to excursion;
We, the hapless few; sad solice in our prayer;
Wisdom knows no recourse to oblivion,
We who shall attempt compromise as our finale,
Must justify endorsement of our dreams to counter –
Balance the whims of our coddled minds.

Cram all excellence into confused contempt,
Strive ever more for preponderance of design;
Fortuitous chasms display depths designed for fate.
As humans we obey a whim of honest plight,
A faith that's led by mightier souls than we.

Forever; in an opaque tomb, desirous of a glimpse of light,
We shine, opalescent with ignominy, lust and contemptible fortune,
We compromise the fruits of our desires;
Bubbling through; sanctimonious; unctuous; fortuitous, exemplory;
Goading and tempting in our path of fervour,
Our way: our existence; such havoc to our minds.

Still, victims we to fortunes bitter gall.
Aye – A wretched vetch knows better what we do,
Knows a peace of mind anew; we claim all, but
Always deny what we are – in carnage, ambivalent,
Silent to what we do not understand; suspicious of what we
comprehend; doubtful of the existence we portray.

The gut rolls; the epitomy of the
Patronising peasant; lower echelons of mediocrity,
Their shadows in these times of economic strife –
Snoop; indeed provoke a confrontational academic
Second of an intellectual's unaccountable time.

They: the miserable wretches; enforce civil laws.
Stinking of quaffings of the previous eve – red eyes;
Their duty to perform: Master's men unwittingly
Alien in all but shape and bioform.

The bailiff; duty quite unperturbed by morals,
Ethics – immaterial in this depressed isle;
Feelings, calculated by cost; charge; debt –
Even corpses lie benign on mortuaries proverbial slab,
Whilst undertakers haggle over unpaid burial debts.

Beehive – the town hall of this cluttered
Bureaucratic little town; Mayoral pomp extruded abroad;
Council leans to argument; emphatic as always,
This land is so important to some foreign fields.
Beware of having faith in alien friends; their costs are high.

This capital, this Cardiff, my demonical demise,
She shrinks before my glassy stare:
She; enveloped in a coal face of surprise,
Her dotage – her hinterland alone, to love and care.

She; void of this claim; forlorn; oblivious;
A carcass in a pool of venom foul;
A capital without a bleeding ediface,
The castle lions simply bear their teeth and growl.

Animals 'midst battlements; stolid effigies,
Portcullis open jawed – more animated now;
Inhabitants seem bound in endless eulogy,
Shadows hang from walls, like holy, charismatic vows.

This queen; at present echoes shrilling horns;
Endless labyrinth of measured gangs of cars,
Traffic of this time, spewing gases, so forlorn,
Mirrored eyes, rubber feet, bloodless battle scars.

Earth, reflective of toil, of Welsh strife,
Seeks, but fails to satiate contention, ambiguity.
Continued usurpment of a Welshman's chiselled life,
A start, fetishist impress of incongruity.

Caerdydd, Sir Morgannwg; do not relent,
Bear with this vestige of the past:
As Welsh patience spills are spent,
We know we'll be here, purblind to the last.

DARTS IN A RHONDDA PUB
WALES

Seldom are the valley's lights so dim;
Man, suit, tie – sleek silken shirt –
Swivels his bulky buttock onto Taiwanese stool,
To wend his daily passage into his other, alcoholic life.

First; tradition, metabolism,
Demand replenishment for his hours of grimy toil.
The boys wait, the 'King's Head' sign swings with gleeful approval,
Jenkins is home, transitory yes, but home.

A glass is filled, raised – its contents disappear.
Watchful eyes decide in silence who replenishes the round.
'Dai'': three hundred and four – the command is obeyed.
A round is ordered on the journey to the board.

The game – in apparent oblivion – is played.
The scorer; only for the time he scores, the Master.
Three darts, three hearty gulps, perhaps a visit,
Soon one loathes this place 'mongst other swilling folk,

Jenkins kept his winning form;
Administered adeptly both rounds, visits and inconclusive chats;
Foremen must be mentioned, bosses discussed, wives criticised.
All forgotten at the dawning of the new repetitive day.

Compunctions; affidavits of a minions course,
Seldom is soliloquy evident; prosaic of mind.
He who runs a somewhat plain remorse,
Echoes deeply of a sombre, different kind.

He cannot wander 'mongst the forests bleak,
Cravings his, erstwhile to crawl and creep;
Languishings these of turgid, waxen type;
Persuasions felt; ignored, but in some ways alike –
The cudgels of a rampart, raucus beast;
Procured pervasions deprivate this melancholic feast.

Ignoble triumphs occupy the vacancies of thought.
Nights pass, oblivious of all teachings that reflect
That inner hope; that yearning for a presence that is thwart;
A search for answers to this world's demise – neglect.
Answers glint through celestial phosphorescent skies,
Each glimpse excites – like babies with their toys.
Seldom is intrinsic egotism, sheltered from itself,
This belly of desire, its flatulence a curse –
Repugnance, wasted fat, with bones that intersperse.

BRECNOCK (WALES)

Sombre shades; low, grim greys,
Brecnock granite glints – that lustre so unique,
Craggy crests merge with slinky swirling mist,
Climbers hasten their descent, lest they too are lost;
Streaks of water; raping the air, aye, depleting all around;
Heather, moss and liverwort, alert, vivid, verdant,
Irridescent yet omnipotent; overshadowing all.

Sepulchral morass, dissipates with elan,
Sun stretches persistently through mercurial mist,
Cold climbers compromising weather's temperament,
Climb to witness Wales; seven counties at a glance.*
A scene of mystical serenity; unique; profound,
Septimal glimpses most find sublime, nostalgic,
This place within a Welshman's repertoire.

* Prior to County Changes

TRIBUTE TO NEW ZEALAND

SALMON RUSHDIE

Western palms, Thatcherites; moralists; purists – all play
Their woeful ploys; Condemnation now in
Vogue; trade – oh so circumspect – in doubt;
Seen to be so moral; so benign – yet
Rushdie's sole expletive is contempt.

The wrath of Allah – total substitute for
Diplomatic puppetry – void of sense. So pompous,
So arrogant – At least New Zealand
Stands alone. May Allah bless the
Wisdom of Lange – How magnificent
Now is David's international repute.

Broken but never bent; David stands alone
'Gainst evils of atomic split; the champion of
Pacific briny isles. Lange alone saw no
Reason to condemn; Muslims, Islam – note well –
This honest man is not afraid to stand his ground,
Whilst British diplomats cry noises so bereft.

Lange's independent stance; A New Zealand once
Again with voice so shrill; Independent will – so
Admired by Ayotollah's wise analogy of Islam.
May Allah bless you for the might of what you've done.

PERPETRATOR
SALMON RUSHDIE

Tauhid – That rock of Islam;
Namaz, that principle so fundamental;
That duty, Farz last doubt beset
A mind; bend in obedience to his Commandments,
Believers; shun not your duty – Men can
Only have peace through the remembrance of Allah.
All good deeds done by tongue, by body and
By money, are purely for the pleasure of Allah.

In the Holy Quran its stated, "Those who
Believe (in the Holy Quran) and the Jews, and the
Christians, and the Sabians, whoever believes in
Allah and in the Last Day, and does that which is
Right, they shall certainly have their reward
From their Lord (in this life or in the hereafter).
No fear shall come upon them, nor shall they grieve.

Rushdie; may Allah tolerate the mention of
Satan's earthly name – you have evoked wrath afar.
"We gave Jesus, son of Mary, clear signs, and
We strengthened Him with the Holy Spirit",
You, Rushdie have mocked the very fabric of the Holy.

IT IS YOUR RIGHT TO DIE
SALMON RUSHDIE

Rave and writhe; There's nothing new to that;
All religion rummages into callous deeds;
The Irish – slaughter is the mask
Of hatred they imbibe; Soviets – released from demise,
Theirs to practice now; but not without regrets.

Catholic, Anglican, Orthodox – Allah, knows you
All so well. Islamic Rights; its virtues;
Faith, Allah, few know of Islam's proclamation.
We have our right; to exorcise our will is right indeed –
We'll only rise again and march to death once more.

Hypocrites who dare to challenge our parade;
A thousand million led by earthly leaders
Striving in the perpetual silent shadow of His making,
As maggots hatched by Satan's aggressive form.
Rushdie; he knows the cost; proclaimed the anti Christ;
Anti Muhammed – appears he the angel of satanic squalor.

As a martyr – death appears your only fortune,
Your only self inflicted right. Doubtless you who meant no
Insult, therefore showed such naivety, such insensitivity,
For one who proclaims such affinity with the Muslim faith;
Perhaps in forgiveness, freedom as you know it,
May once again be yours.

INSIGNIFICANCE PERSONIFIED
ON SALMON RUSHDIE

You, Rushdie, may never speak the truth,
Your retirement years now accountable.
Allah, so well acquainted with unjust people; Ye who
Benignly talk of Satan; A party threw the word
Of Allah to the Wind: They followed the Devil –
Against the Kingdom of Solomon – accursed is
The price for selling off those Souls.

To Allah belong the east and west;
Therefore whatever direction you turn yourselves,
You find the presence of God who is all–pervading,
All knowing; everything therein is obedient
To Him, listen well all those collusive seekers of "Satanic Verses".
Allah said "My covenant does not
Embrace the unjust and ungodly people".

What have you tried Rushdie? Are you a despot?
A filthy inhuman carnage of unrequited lust –
Why flirt with stench? So oblivious
Of contempt; congealed canker; so mentally corrupt –
Perhaps insane? You empty out, disembowelling the
Very pith of prophesy; futile attempts to smear, doubt;
To impose your own pitiful pittance on their noble selves.
Death, not for you or your insignificance.
You don't deserve death;
The root of good, the semblance of faith, you must live
Free, possibly to justify, explain your perhaps
Unintentional naive encounter with a people's soul.

IMANIYAT
(Faith)

'Oh My Servants! remember me, and I will
Remember you; and give thanks to Me and do
Not be ungrateful to Me'.
'Wherever you are, Allah is with you;
'Verify, he hears and sees'.

Again you must believe that He is the first, He
Is the last and He is the Outward and the
Inwards; and he is the Knower of all things,
The Holy Quran teaches us.

'And then, at last, we should also believe
That this, is a Day of Judgement when a
Complete record of all good or bad deeds
Done by us, will be given in our hands. And who
So doeth good, an atom's weight see it then.
And who so doeth ill, an atom's weight will see it then'.

And when a person has such a Faith, how can
He commit any kind of sin? And, when there
Is no sin in the world, how can there be
Confusion, cruelty, disorder or misery of any nature?
Islam wants to form such a society; I think that
Every reasonable and sensible person would like to help this cause.

THE CATHERINE WHEEL OF FATE

The Anti Muhammed – The Antichrist

Islam – except not the poisoned dart of tongue
So dismal is it anecdote; Islam – our undisputed
Life blood; We who embrace Islam, with all it is –
We who from the dungeons of our hearts
Know that incandescent self; that fundamental
Fact; No one is worthy of worship but Allah,
Muhammed is a True Prophet of Him.

Filth from the little men; those whose pitiful
Exchange; whose hunted poisonous darts fall
Omnipotent; pallid; lifeless – bounced back on sandy
Soil – infertile, unrepenting – hollow in their wanton
Futile mediocrity; Their intended message,
As always is the Devil's plight – thwarted,
Indeed vanquished; buried 'neath an infallible Islam.

Rushdie, as you shiver in contemplation of
Your erstwhile plight; Take heed my niggard knight,
My catherine wheel of fate: Allah! you are Peace
Personified; you are the course of peace for all;
Oh Allah, Oh Creator, let us enter the Home of
Peace – per chance Rushdie's insult may not be avenged
In this fleeting lifetime – so miniscule in the millennium of time.

ETAKADAT
(Islamic Faith)

The curse of Allah be on you, Rushdie
Also all your potentates, your scribes, your
Fickle friends; Opportunists in political scrums and rucks.
Politicians play semantics – like fuddled fools,
So naive – concerned, castration of a crass market,
Left to lesser infidels; to maggots of their testy
Apoplectic Cabinet's inept demise.

Remonstrations: so hollow; ignorance sublime;
The curse of Allah be on disbelievers – "Where
To them who corruptly transcribe the book of Law,
That they may sell it for a small price. Woe to
Them for what they gain thereby! The fire of hell may not
Touch you for a small number of days – you who care,
Encompassed by their iniquity; you are now the
Inmate of Fire – and shall remain therein for ever.

Rushdie! your kith; your kin; shall scream. We of
Islam; We gave Moses the Book and caused a train
Of messengers to follow in these footsteps. We gave
Jesus, Son of Mary, clear signs, miracles.
We strengthened Him with the Holy Spirit – the Archangel
Gabriel. Allah will curse you for your infidelity,
For you have sold your soul. You shall now be humiliated,
By your own conscience and the will of Allah.

LISTEN WELL RUSHDIE

Hypocrisy know you well; you, a stable mate.
Anger, spite and envy, bedfellow of presumption,
Egoism innovative of faith.

How well you breach promise; How fickle at embezzlement,
Aggravated obscenity and hollow, shallow talk.

Pitiful your encompassment of time, travel;
Forbidding Zakat, Charity, Haj and its requirements.

Neighbour's right you have raped; adultery,
Disobedience of a parent's respect; Curse and
Rejection of a faith you fail to comprehend.

To you, vesper of shame; as you
Violate the commands of Allah.
Interdiction to evaluate.

Throw askance the thought of human blood relationship.
Discourtesy, your Satan's relentless pledge;
Murder; suicide; seemingly your parishes once more.

That white enclave; that immersed Walkabout,
Insincerity; seemingly the only answer for this isolation.
Rife apartheid in this large, ignominious, racialistic, continent.
The proud tribal aboriginal – a culture, a heritage;
Far superior to the Maori or the patronising whites,
Who sell the booze – adding easy profits.
To takings for the day.

Not satisfied – hyperactive Aboriginals disgorge western swill.
Khaki garbed; silver epauletted, crown – buttoned whites,
Toss bags of stinking, human flesh aboard
Polished Toyotas, wire cages abaft, not for rabid dogs.

Holding cells – strewn with layers of Australians – Aboriginals,
Paying penance for imbibing white man's booze,
Liquids, not of their design – a scene oft
Repeated throughout colonial lands;
The white man has the key. He always turns it full.

No wonder how little, James Gallaway cares for me –
At dawn, next day, he srolls away.
My assistant, gone walkabout with alcoholic friends,
Keen to turn the cheek – he has no respect here.
As a graduate of Bible College he finds
The bilingualism, western influence; and peer pressures
Too great; alcohol and Winfield now his closest pals.

Like the white man in South Africa; The Australian
Of a differing ethnic race is treated as trash, messy, a 'wog'
He's fed on white man's junk. Why should white man care.
If liquor, nicotine or sugar, thrust upon these naive folk,
Rips their existence apart, conveniences of their
Dwindling members, helps the whites to bury their embarrassment.

DOOMSDAY

Seldom will that cloudless dawn,
Figurative in its furtive struggle:
Benign yet welcome in the stamen of the sun,
Somnambulant; yet restless in the clasp of time.

He seems so eloquent, unprovoked;
We know he seldom sees a theme outcast;
In closer content a text is promulgated –
Proclaiming yet another tranquil, transient day.

Our power, so infinitesimal in the Universal Plan,
Yet; our balance upset by nuclear potential,
Environmental disease, placing perspective awkwardly askew;
One man literally holding power to destroy all.

FIJI
*RAMBUKA'S PERILOUS PRETENCE

Fiji – its patience now deplete,
Conscious of its glorious sun and surf.
Resplendent in its majesty and beauty
Gathering whispers on its hallowed swords and turf.

Fiji's right to Fiji is like coconut to palm,
The people of this carefree land
To others present, mean no harm.
Fijians, proud to serve their Queen, have suffered hand in hand.

Connivances by alien folk,
Whose objectives aren't denied,
Their threats to commerce, industry,
Forget Fijian's native enterprise.

Fijian culture; this is theirs,
Not sold in trade or package deals;
Exchange of hopes, ideas, plans,
Their fate is quite uniquely sealed.

Pretender to Fiji's throne will know,
Intention's path is ritually steep,
For him, his racial overtones, must be, for Fiji's sake,
Always deep in sleep.

* Colonel Rambuka led the 1989 coup in Fiji. The democratically elected
government was ousted at gunpoint whilst sitting in Parliament

IRRELIGIOUS
THE BAR OF I

Each hour is spent whistling pleasant tunes,
But many hours of bliss will wallow still.
A tavern's door; pitted; a studded design of pleasures, thirsts,
A sturdy barrier this to unfrequented lust –
A whore standing; a silhouette to offerings of kind 'gainst oak.

Some dubious, naked parson; cautious of his flock,
Will not be chaste before this day is o'er;
We find a happy band of followers in our midst,
This bar of discontent is stout and tough:
Colossus sees a peace dream collapsed.

This frigid lust for fellowship seems undetermined, lost;
Its very plot seems circumspect; irrelevant; incandescent,
To whimsical distractions of a Mass; a ceremony of like minds.
Oh! Seasons of our thoughts; patterned , parlous pans, mosaic
Strategies; magnificent in plan; obsequious – disarranged;
Yet seemingly profound.

That constant alcoholic swill enters cavities of the brain;
Clarity numbed; truth confounded, contrived; the human mind,
Usurped of discernment and wholesome zeal.
A church door; pitted; studded design of establishment;
Sturdy barrier to unsolicited alms of persons unknown;
The parson, like the whore, here to satiate repentance;
Their damnation rescinded through acceptance of the norm.

The bar of discontent: The reasons for mind's mental tides,
Confused amidst ebb and flow; now usurp the mind again.

Some fetid site; some putrid fool –
Whole armies fight – conditioned to conform;
Lights of chance glimmer in subterranean cells.
Faith often plays its reliable, ready role –
Cathode screens relate opinion of those close:
That media; ever greedy for that bloodier scene,
Scoops – envied by both editor and cub.

One element, so assuring in the promises they make,
The lowliest forms of life decide.
The 'germ' in a multitude of hostile pathogenic forms,
No dam, no food, no blood, no beast,
Is safe from bacterial strike –
Nature in its many ways,
Always wins with subterfuge,
On this – or any day.

EROTICISM

Unbridled kiss of night against my will –
Lie they buried; churlish echoes of a night so still;
Tangled gossamers waft nocturnal scents astray,
My love; she's repentant excuse; passion so potent ne'r portrayed.

> Though lover's depths are deep,
> Eddies, currents – oft effect their sleep.

Come, my love; exhilarate my lust,
Lest by quirk of fortune it is laid to dust;
Let you and I relent to erotic graceful ways,
My passion; cravings – released; not turned to clay.

> Harmonious, as tides reverse their flow,
> Gratuitous as ocean's pearls to swine would know.

IS THAT ME

I know I'm me
I think I'm me
It seems like me
This is me.

Am I me?
Can I see me?
Is this me?
This is me!

My mirror shows me
That is me
This is me?
No that is me

It may be me
It could be me
That's me
I can see that
It is me.

I know it's me
I think I'm me
It seems it's me – but
This is me

This is me?
Yes – this is me.

WINKLES

Shells crackle under shoes
Sticks crack under me
I am heavy – trod, trod

Leaves crunch under shoes
Cans crimple under me
I am heavy – plod, plod

Brittle dry forests – dark
Green greens of the park
I am heavy – crush, crush.

Grass green, green, green,
In each damp place
I crush – I am heavy, heavy.

Sheltered places, moss clings, clings, clings;
Water holes, water falls – toadstool rings,
I make mud – slither, slip, slip
Sand slips under me.

I'm too heavy now
I'm too heavy – sink, sink, sink.

POLES

A way to prove
   The world's not square
      Is to ask a wise
         Old Polar Bear –
            For it is likely
               He'll agree
                  That his home is inside 360
                     degrees

He certainly is too cold to ponder
   He has no time to sit and wonder
      He'll stare and nod his head at you
         Wondering whether you're mad or rude
            But after he's coaxed with a fish or two
               You'll probably find he's quite bemused.

The world is round
That's quite profound
For there is a CIRCLE
All around.

GHOST ON TOAST

He lived in my toast
  I loved him the most
    As I crunched away
      He'd look up and say
        Crunch Crunch Crunch

        I'd put egg on his face
          Down his cheek it would race
            As I crunched away
              He'd stare up and say
                Munch Munch Munch

                He lived in my toast
                  And I loved him the most
                    As I munched away
                      He'd happily say

                        I'm your Ghost

MY STAR

At the centre of the sky,
You always find a star.
It might seem close or far away,
By bus or train or car.

No train or plane or ship or bike,
Can reach my sparkling prize.
It's sometimes hidden by the clouds
In black ferocious skies.

My star is special, 'mine' – my own,
It always seems too much alone.
It nudged the moon the other day
The moon just pushed it right away.

Moon, stars, capsules and shuttles,
Satellites, orbits, rockets and stations,
Space seems to relish this hustle and bustle.
But my star remains – in imagination.

ADAM'S DISTANT THOUGHTS ON FRISBIES

He wriggled and tickled and giggled and bumped,
Each tickle was riddled with various thumps,
His giggles and wriggles and tickles were real,
To him, they all had a most ticklish feel.

As he scrambled downstairs on a fine Sunday morn,
Carrying Squiggles – his bear – all tattered and torn,
He wandered outside where his frisby lay still,
He wondered and wondered 'bout travels and thrills.

Mist hung in wisps around trees in his yard,
The frost and cold made everything hard,
Mummy was clanking the pots and the pans,
Hot porridge and toast, would soon be at hand,

He looked at his frisby and asked it in vain,
Had it flown to the Arctic, the moon – or to Spain?
Where had it been, on that cold starry night?
What was it really like, up there in flight?

He went in for breakfast, hot toast and honey,
Thinking of space travels, away from his mummy.
Home was so good and he thought that it may,
Be better than journeys to lands far away.

ON CATS

A watchful eye spots in a flash
The running, fleeting glimpse of rat,
Somewhat large for Brandy cat.
He senses movements large and small,
Especially if he hears the call,
Of some small innocent bird or beast,
He thinks might make a sumptuous feast.

Brandy Snaps – full title please!
Seems inclined to live at ease.
A royal; a stylish pace in life,
Why shouldn't he enjoy a slice,
Of the very best of things,
Like field mice, bats and things with wings?

He glances 'round from on his perch,
A piece of orchard there to search,
For hated things like boys next door,
The very thought turns tongue to paw;
Those dogs, those slings, those water hoses,
Things to spoil life's 'Bed of roses'.

Last night, just as the master said,
'He's scratched up seeds from my seed bed'.
After all – everyone knows,
What comes in – out the other end goes;
Is he supposed to know they're seeds?
Why he'd be thanked if they were weeds!

Between the dogs and boys' of prey,
There's nowhere peaceful left to stay.
After all – two legged beasts or four,
Are really just a tiresome bore;
What's that! Ah ha! his butler's called,
"I wonder what's for dinner Paul?"

He thinks he'll choose the other chair,
The master never sits down there.
It's so near the roasting fire,
So welcome when one's bones are tired;
He thinks he'll sleep and dream all night,
Of fish, meat and felines slight.

He wishes you a restful night.

Mousetraps: they have springs and
Other coiling kinds of things.
Doors, they have their hinges,
Bees and wasps their stings.
Bugs, they have antennae,
Butterflies have wings,
Birds have little claws
Which grip tight onto things.

> But me, I have a shadow that
> Goes everywhere with me,
> From my playground to my bedroom
> Just as everyone can see.

Snails: have spiral houses,
They are slimy kinds of things.
Toadstools have umbrellas,
That make funny kinds of rings.
Bats, they live in belfries,
Hidden well from daylight's glare,
Owls have huge round saucer eyes,
At everything, they stare.

> But me, I have a shadow that
> Goes everywhere with me,
> From my playground to my bedroom
> Just as everyone can see.

You see he is my shadow, made especially by me.

KING GOLLUP

Of dreary dungeons he is King,
Around his huge and ugly form,
There glows a light like early morn.
His servants – toads and crawling beasts
Prepare with care his sumptuous feasts.
Ants and bees and crocodiles
He gollups down in King-like style.
His eyes bright green – watch every move,
For every day he has to prove
That he's the Gollup of them all,
The mightiest – upright, bold and tall.

Gollupians – beasts so loyal and true,
Know all the deeds that they must do.
Travelling under roots and rocks,
Working right around the clock,
Digging caverns dark and damp,
Without a shovel, pick or lamp.
A Gollup must be kept in style,
His boots so shiny, his teeth kept filed.
A Gollup's life is very long –
And we all know, he's never wrong,
The Gollup has the final say
Each morning, evening and all day.

At half past five – by Gollup time,
The Gollup yawns – to clear his mind.
A day to plan and schemes to scheme,
How to be cunning and cruel and mean.
'My breakfast! calls out King to toad –
Fiendish snakes arrive in loads.
As Gollup lies in royal style,
In march toads in single file.
Ant's eggs, lizards, bees and beasts,
Prepared with care the royal feast,

All golluped down by half past nine –
Four hours of feasting and gulping wine.

And then – as all Gollupians know,
Their king likes putting on a show.
Beneath that chest of matted hair,
There lurks a heart that can be fair.
At least to some his rules make sense
And after all he's not too dense;
To realise and understand,
That he must be seen as Charge d'affaires,
He has no time for love or care.

Gollupians you must soldier on,
His day will end and he'll be gone.